Card Play
or, The Truth About the Knave of Hearts

A play for young people

David Foxton

Samuel French – London
New York – Sydney – Toronto – Hollywood

ISBN 0 573 15005 2

Please see page iv for further copyright information

CHARACTERS

2D, the Two of Diamonds
6D, the Six of Diamonds
Jack Smart, the Knave of Hearts
Myra, the Two of Hearts
Q, the Queen of Spades
Jackson, the Five of Spades
Jack Flash (Shiner), the Knave of Diamonds
QH, the Queen of Hearts
4D, the Four of Diamonds
3D, the Three of Diamonds
10C, the Ten of Clubs
2S, the Two of Spades
KH, the King of Hearts
5D, the Five of Diamonds
6H, the Six of Hearts ⎫
7H, the Seven of Hearts ⎬ Guards/attendants

ACT I   Behind the scenes/dressing area of a large sports stadium
ACT II   Outside and later inside *The Bridge Club*—a night club
ACT III   As Act I

ACT I

Behind the scenes/dressing area of a large sports stadium. The rear of the area is labelled with hearts, clubs, diamonds and spades

The Two of Diamonds (2D) enters, backwards

2D (*shouting off*) See if I care! It's all right for you, isn't it? Oh yes! But I'm fed up . . . right up to here I'm fed up. I said "I'm fed up". You're not listening to me. (*Shouting*) I said "You're not listening to me". (*He is sulky now*) It's always the same. I'm always the one left out of the game. (*He shouts off*) And it's not fair! It's just because I'm a two . . . they're always taking advantage of me. (*He shouts off*) I can't help being a two! And you're still not listening. (*He sits and picks up the paper*) Look at that . . . "Big Match Special!" "Reds to Win?" "A Close Game Expected". Oh yes! Of course it'll be close . . . what else does it say? "Confident of the line up that he announced today." Where's that, let me see . . . Diamonds— 10, 9, 8, 6, 5 . . . Hearts—Ace, 9, 8, 7 . . . I'm not even on the list! Where's the reserves? Four of Diamonds and Three of Hearts . . . I'm not even there. It's all here in the paper! Announced in the paper and I didn't know . . . I turn up here all ready to play and I'm left out . . . again! (*A pause as he reads the paper*) It's every time the same you know . . . every single blooming time—does it happen to you? I keep being left out. If anyone has to go it's always me. "Get rid of the Two of Diamonds," they all say. I'm always being discarded . . . hey, d'you get that, dis—*card*—ed . . . me a card . . . a . . . oh, forget it! I wish I was a six, or a seven, I'd show 'em. What does me horoscope say . . . let's see what's predicted . . . "Cookery Competition—Queen of Hearts Announces Prizes." That's not it! "Suspect at large." That's not it! "Crossword" . . . that's not it . . . just my luck isn't it . . . there's no horoscopes, no star signs . . . how will I know what to expect? Anything could happen to me now!

The Six of Diamonds (6D) staggers on, holding his/her head which is bleeding a little

2D My word! Are you all right? What on earth happened to you.
6D I've been trumped.
2D Pardon?
6D I've been trumped! There I was, just about to win this trick for our side, when suddenly before you could say "canasta" I was trumped by one of the Clubs.
2D It looks as though you were "clubbed" by one of the trumps!
6D Oh, very funny! Anyway, it amounts to the same thing.
2D Sit down. Let's have a look at your injury.

6D sits down

Oh dear! Oh dearie me!

6D What is it? Is it serious?

2D No ... I don't know ... it's just that I can't stand the sight of blood. I feel a bit wobbly all over. Get up and let me sit down.

However they both sit side by side

(*Moaning*) Oooh!

6D Give over. I'm the one that's hurt.

2D It's sympathy.

6D It's not ... it's hypochondria!

2D (*standing*) How dare you! How dare you! What a thing to say. Now I really am hurt. What does it mean anyway?

6D It means that *I'm* ill and *you're* pretending to be ill.

2D Oh *that* hypochondria. Why didn't you say so?

They sit side by side. Pause

Doesn't it feel any better at all?

6D A bit.

2D Nasty thing, being trumped.

6D I'll say.

2D Who's winning then?

6D What?

2D I said, "who's winning then?"

6D Who do you think?

2D Us?

6D No ... try again.

2D (*pausing while he thinks*) Er ... *them*!

6D Well done! Oh very well done! Of course they're winning—don't they always? I've played almost every game, every single game—and each time our side loses. The Clubs and Spades always win.

2D I didn't know that.

6D It's amazing really. I don't know how they do it. Just when you think the tricks are really going your way, then suddenly you're behind.

2D What about it?

6D Behind, in the game!

2D Oh ... I wasn't playing.

6D We had a chance to be top of the league, and now where are we?

2D Where indeed!

6D And now, today, we'll be out of the cup if we're not careful. Then where would we be?

2D In the saucer?

6D Can't you be serious for once? It's no wonder the manager doesn't pick *you* to play. You *twos* are all the same. I'm going to get my head seen to.

6D exits

2D Oh yes ... I'd do that. I reckon your head *needs* seeing to ... from the inside! (*To the audience*) Did you hear that? "You twos are all the same."

'Course we are! What else could we be? (*He shouts off*) You sixes are all the same too! And the sevens! It's obvious isn't it? Listen, I'll let you into a secret. *I'm* not the only two on our side ... no! There's two of us. Look! Look! It's in the paper ... on the team list ... just have a look ... see! There—under the Hearts ... 9, 8, 7, 6, 5, 4, 2. The *two* of Hearts. But the manager doesn't like *me*. Whenever somebody has to be left out, it's always *me*. "Get rid of the Two of Diamonds," he says—never the Two of Hearts. Oh no! I reckon he fancies her. Old Jack, Jack Smart, our Manager—he always picks *her*. I wouldn't trust him an inch. Sly he is! "We have a strong hand," said Smart earlier today ... hah! How can it be ... with the Two of Hearts in it! And leaving *me* out?

The Knave of Hearts (Jack Smart), the Manager, enters with the Two of Hearts (Myra)

Jack Smart Steady! Steady! How are you feeling now?

Myra I'll be all right, Jack, don't worry. Did it look good?

Jack Smart Beautiful, darling, beautiful. It really looked very good. When you went down the crowd roared ... I thought you really were hurt.

2D Hello Boss!

Jack Smart (*surprised*) What? Who is it? Blimey—don't do things like that! I didn't know you were there ... creeping up on us that way. Can't you see I'm coping with ... with ... an injury problem here.

Myra faints noisily

Now look. I don't know whether she'll be able to go on again. (*He pats her hands and face*) Are you all right? There, there, Jack's here ... are you all right, Myra?

Myra moans

2D What happened, Boss?

Jack Smart Happened? Happened? I'll tell you what happened. She was brought down, wasn't she? One of the worst trumpings I've ever seen. Vicious it was ... uncalled for. No retaliation involved ... just callous, plain callous ... he ought to have gone. He ought to be off by now! But oh no! Oh no! There's no justice! And here's one of my best, my very best cards ... and I can't play her. (*He turns back to minister to her*) There! There!

2D (*to the audience*) Didn't I tell you that he liked her. Didn't I say? "One of my best cards." She's a *two* ... like me! It's not fair ... it's unjust and ... rotten ... and awful. I'll never play now. I'll not play even if he got down on his bended knees and begged me. If it was the World Cup I wouldn't play. Never, never, never.

Jack Smart There's nothing for it. You'll just have to go on.

2D Never in a month of Sundays. Never in a year of half-day closings ...

Jack Smart Stop talking to yourself and listen to me. You've got to go on. You've got to play ...

2D So you can keep your team. Keep 'em. I don't want any part of it. You can ... what did you say?

Jack Smart I said you're on . . . *now*. Get playing . . . what are you waiting for?

2D Yahoo! Here I go! This is it. Here I come. Watch out for the whizz kid.

2D exits singing the "Match of the Day" tune

Jack Smart (*shouting off*) Watch out for their number ten . . . he's wicked he is!

Myra (*recovering*) Do you think that was wise, Jack?

Jack Smart Wise?

Myra To send him on.

Jack Smart Well, we needed him out of the way, didn't we? We didn't want him here . . . did we, my love?

Myra Don't give me that "my love" bit. We didn't want him here, and we didn't want him out there. I thought you'd sent him away.

Jack Smart I had! I did! I told him there was no place for him—but he wouldn't take "no" for an answer. But he's out of the way now.

Myra But for how long?

Jack Smart How long?

Myra How long before he gets trumped out there? One of those clubs'll have him before he knows where he is . . . then he'll be back here.

Jack Smart He'll last a few minutes.

Myra Well, I hope he does for *your* sake.

Jack Smart What do you mean by that?

Myra I mean we don't want disturbing when "you know who" arrives do we? So let's hope that the Two of Dumbos stays on his feet and out of trouble until we've finished here.

The Five of Spades (Jackson) enters

Jackson Is it clear?

Jack Smart What?

Jackson Can she come in? Now?

Jack Smart Oh yeah! Sure thing! We're . . . er . . . all ready.

Jackson We don't want no trouble.

Jack Smart Certainly not.

Jackson Right!

Jackson exits

Myra Do you know what you're going to ask for?

Jack Smart Ask for?

Myra Our share! What's our cut going to be?

Jack Smart Fifty-fifty?

Myra And don't you forget it!

Jackson enters with the Queen of Spades (Q)

Jackson It's all clear, Boss!

Q Keep a look out, Jackson.

Jackson Will do, will do (*He adopts a look-out pose*)

Q Now then . . . to business.

Jack Smart Ready when you are . . . blue eyes!

Q Let's get things clear shall we, from the beginning. *I* run this whole outfit. Right?

Jack Smart Sure . . . sure . . . Of course you're right.

Q When a game is on. Like now! I call all the shots! And *my* team wins!

Jack Smart But of course, Q, of course what else could it be?

Q So my team *always* wins! And your team always loses! Do I make myself clear?

Jack Smart Clear indeed!

Myra As crystal.

Q And I don't need comments from you. So keep quiet! Understood?

Jack Smart Understood. (*He nudges Myra*)

Myra Of course, anything you say.

Q We win because I cheat. Fairness is not a word I understand.

Jack Smart Nor me! Nor me!

Q I intend to take over the whole pack of you—and only those who go along with my ideas will survive: am I getting through to you?

Jack Smart Oh yes! Yeah! You are, you are.

Q And I've dealt with some difficult knaves in my time, I can tell you. Very difficult ones.

Jack Smart I know! I know!

Q So what's your big idea?

Jack Smart Pardon?

Q I said what's your big idea?

Jack Smart I don't quite follow.

Myra Let me speak, Jack. You must forgive him Q, he's rather overwhelmed by your modesty and charm. But I ain't. The story goes something like this. Things are going reasonably well for us at the moment—and are going *very* well for you. But we think it's time that *we* had a share in the . . . big time.

Jackson See here, ain't you getting just a little too big for your boots?

Q Quiet, Jackson. I can handle this.

Jackson Shall I give her a quick reminder who's boss, Boss?

Q I can handle it, Jackson—you keep your eyes peeled. We don't want any interruptions.

Jackson If you say so, Boss.

Myra Get back on your perch, eagle-eyes!

Jackson Aw, Boss! Let me give her a little reminder.

Q Later Jackson, later.

Jack Smart Don't mix it, Myra!

Q Good advice, Jack; good advice.

Jack Smart Myra didn't mean to be pushy, Q. It's right what she said though—*we* want a piece of the action.

Q Do you?

Myra And we have an idea that'll bring us that piece.

Q Have you?

Jack Smart But we'll need your support.

Q Will you?

Jackson Don't have any dealings with these guys. **Boss.** You can't trust "Reds"—they're all the same. We're on top, and we mean to stay there.

Q There's truth in what you say, Jackson. But let's hear what their idea is. Who knows, we may be able to make use of it ourselves.

Myra No way. You'll need us. Without our help it can't be done.

Q Tell us what it is.

Jack Smart So you're interested?

Q I am ... somewhat intrigued.

Jack Smart and Q exchange glances

So, speak.

Jack Smart It's like this ...

6D enters, bandaged

6D There ... look, as good as new. I'll be able to go back on if necessary. I'll show that big number ten ... Oh, sorry, excuse me! I didn't know you were here. Jack! Myra! And ... hey, what are you two doing here? You're the opposing side.

Jack Smart It's all right, Six. Nothing to worry about ... it's all all right.

6D But I don't understand. They're the opposition—that's Q herself. Jack, what's going off here?

Jack Smart Discussions—that's all—discussions.

6D I don't like the sound of it.

Jackson Shall I give him the works, Boss?

Q Not yet Jackson, not yet!

6D What are they doing here?

Myra There's nothing illegal going off ...

Jack Smart Don't mix it, Myra!

6D And what are you doing here? Why aren't you out there?

Myra I was very badly injured ...

6D Oh yes. You look *very* badly injured.

Jack Smart Listen, Six, listen. I think perhaps that knock you took ...

6D Don't give me that.

Jackson Now Boss? Can I get him now?

Q Wait! All of you. Now listen to me. Six is it?

6D Course it's Six. (*Pointing to his diamonds*) What do you think these are? And anyway, it's Six of Diamonds to you.

Q You don't have to take that attitude with me. You don't have to be so aggressive, you don't have to be so suspicious.

Jack Smart Not at all.

Myra There's nothing going off.

Pause

6D I don't believe you.

Q Listen. I can help you. You've had an injury, I see. It could mean that you might not play for some time.

Myra It could be serious ...

Jack Smart Might mean a long lay off, Six.

Q And you'd be short of cash, no doubt. Now I could help there. If you were to forget about this little meeting today. I could see that you were amply rewarded.

Pause

6D You're trying to bribe me.
Q Oh come now ... to help you, to help all of us.
Jack Smart So what do you say?
Myra Take the money, Six. Think what you could do with it!

Pause

6D So there is something going off! There is something being planned! You are all up to something illegal! I thought it ... I guessed as much. And now I know ... (*pointing to Jack*) ... you ... and her (*pointing to Myra*) ... are working with the other side. That's what it is ... am I right? I am, aren't I? Tell me ... that's it isn't it?
Q Now Jackson, now!

Jackson coshes 6D who collapses. Myra shrieks

Quiet you fool! Now get rid of him, Jackson.

Jackson drags 6D to the rear of the stage

Jackson Anything you say, Boss.
Myra I didn't want any violence!
Jack Smart Don't mix it, Myra!
Q You can't make an omelette without breaking eggs. Now—quickly, what's the job?
Jack Smart Well ... er ... it's ...
Q Come on man. I don't have time.
Jackson He's still breathing, Boss.
Q What was your idea?
Jack Smart Robbery.
Q Is that all?
Jackson (*disappointed*) *Just* a robbery.
Jack Smart A big one.
Myra The *biggest* yet.
Q Tell me ...

Offstage shouts from the crowd

2D (*off*) No, I'm not coming back. He tried to kill me ... he wants to be locked up. He's an animal. You can keep your game.

2D enters, badly torn about and battered

Jackson tries to hide 6D

What a game! Did you see that, Boss? It's not sport that, it's a massacre. It's like General Custard all over again. Did you see it, Two? It's like playing against a team of gorillas. We don't stand a chance. I was knocked over twice before I started playing, talk about being shuffled. No wonder you came off, Two. Are you all right now? Look at me—I'm an absolute wreck . . . I was boxed twice.

During the next Q signals to Jackson to cosh 2D, but he is too elusive, unconsciously moving out of harm's way at the last moment

And I'm almost torn to shreds. (*He shouts off*) I'm not coming back on . . . It's no good waiting for me . . . I told 'em, I said if you're going to play like this then I don't want any part of it. They were playing out of order, cheating, revoking; they wouldn't play fair. I said to that big Ten of Clubs, I said, you may be bigger than me but that doesn't mean I don't have some value, I said. And do you know what he replied, do you? Well I'll tell you. He said, "Cribbage!" I thought, "cribbage" yourself. I mean he shouldn't use language like that . . . during a game. I could see the way the wind was blowing. I tried to keep out of trouble . . . but it's not easy. I mean, we're being annihilated out there. We haven't won a trick for ages. It's soul destroying. So I came off . . . I thought, "get off" before they carry you off. I could end up like Six, I mean did you see his head? Talk about a trumping, what a bashing he took. Well I can tell you, I don't want one of those . . . no thank you very much. He came in here. He was almost out on his feet. There was blood everywhere. I did my best . . . but he was almost beyond help (*He shouts off*) I'm not coming back! I said, "I'm not coming back". You know, I don't think anyone is listening . . . oh look here's Six. My word, he still looks badly . . . I say Six, are you all right old chap? (*He stoops over him*)

Q, Jack Smart, and Myra whisper to each other

Q Tonight! We'll talk at the Bridge Club.
Jack Smart We'll be there.
Q Jackson! Come on.
Myra Jack! Jack! This way.

Jack Smart and Myra exit, the opposite side to Q and Jackson

2D He doesn't seem to be conscious. Give me a hand, will you? He must have had a relapse of some kind. Just lend us a hand . . . I said give us a . . . (*He looks round*) Now that's odd. There were people here a minute ago, I could have sworn there were. And now . . .

6D moans

I'm here, let me give you a hand. That bump you got when you were trumped was worse than you thought. Come on, up you come, come and sit down over here . . . (*He helps 6D forward*) There now, and how are you feeling now? How's the head?
6D Head?
2D Yes, your head. How is your head. (*He pats 6D's head*)
6D Oooh!
2D Oh sorry! It must be a bit tender.
6D Tender?

2D Where you were bumped.
6D Bumped?
2D Oh heck! It's just like talking to the Two of Spades. Are you all right? ALL RIGHT?
6D Who are you?
2D That's better. I thought for a minute you were far away. What do you mean, "who are you?"
6D Where am I?
2D Wait a minute let's deal with one question at a time.
6D What am I doing here?
2D Ah now, there's one I can answer. You see . . .
6D Why were they in here?
2D Who?
6D All of them?
2D I think that bump was worse than we first thought. Did they see to your head . . . in there?
6D Talking . . .
2D Of course I'm talking. What do you think I'm doing—playing patience?
6D Who am I?
2D Oh dear—that's all I need. Don't tell me that you've lost your memory.
6D Lost . . . memory.
2D No, I said *don't* tell me that. That's all I need *you* to have a dose of ambrosia . . .
6D Amnesia.
2D It's where your brain turns to rice pudding—I read about it somewhere. And you don't want to have anything to do with it, it's not good for you. And you won't get any symphony from me.
6D Sympathy.
2D Not a single note. You'll have to pull yourself together, I don't want you getting all compressed.
6D Depressed.
2D It's like being shut in a box, you'll end up with kleptomania.
6D Claustrophobia!

6D grabs 2D

2D Keep your hands to yourself!
6D Claustrophobia! Depression! Sympathy! Amnesia!
2D Never heard of them. They're nowhere around here—I can tell you that for a fact.
6D It's all coming back to me.
2D Well if it sounds as bad as that lot I wouldn't bother.
6D No—listen. Listen . . . I came in here . . .
2D I know I saw you, you'd been trumped . . . and I looked at your head . . .
6D No, no—after that . . . when I came back.
2D Oh, then. I don't think I was here then—was I?
6D And there was . . . let me think . . . it's still very unclear . . . hazy . . . who was here . . .
2D Give me a clue.

Pause. While they think—behind them a character enters furtively—Jack of Diamonds (Jack Flash) or Shiner to his friends

Jack Flash Pssst!

2D Pssst! That's not much of a clue; is it a pentagram?

6D Anagram.

2D Is it. Let's think then . . . what will that make?

Jack Flash Oi! Oi! (*He clicks his fingers*)

2D No! That's no good! Too many O's.

Jack Flash Has it been fixed?

2D I didn't even know it was broken.

Jack Flash Arranged is it?

2D Is it?

Jack Flash That's what I want to know.

2D Don't we all?

Jack Flash You are in the know aren't you?

2D In the what?

Jack Flash *Know. Know.*

2D No! No!

Jack Flash Yes! Yes!

2D All right have it your way. Yes! Yes!

6D A plan . . . a plan with Q.

Jack Flash So you are in the know?

2D Are we?

6D Jack, and . . . Myra . . . were talking to the Queen of Spades in here . . . when I . . . came . . . in.

Jack Flash So it's all organized then is it? We've got the go-ahead have we?

2D Just a minute! Hold everything! I am not following this. I am yards behind. (*To Jack Flash*) Now, tell me, who are you?

Jack Flash Jack o' Diamonds, known usually as Jack Flash. But you can call me "Shiner".

2D Who are you playing for?

Jack Flash I'm on *my* side: look after number one—that's what *I* always say.

6D What are you here for then?

Jack Flash Come on now, you don't have to be careful with me . . . we're all in the same boat, ain't we?

6D Are we?

Jack Flash Listen, you don't need to be suspicious of me. I'm in on it . . . like you.

2D Just a minute, I've heard of you somewhere.

Jack Flash Course you have . . . from herself. From Q.

2D Q?

6D Or course! She was here just now.

Jack Flash That's it. Now you're talking.

2D I must have read it in the paper. Let me see (*He searches for the paper and then the item*)

6D Yes . . . I think I understand now.

Jack Flash I thought you did.

6D Look ... er ... Shiner ... just nip outside a minute and ... er ... check whether it's half-time yet. We don't want to be interrupted do we? Know what I mean?

Jack Flash Oh sure! Sure! Right then. I won't be two ticks.

Jack Flash exits

2D Here it is. Look here. "Information would still be appreciated concerning the whereabouts of the Knave of Diamonds, also known as Jack Flash and 'Shiner' in criminal circles." Shiner. That was him.

6D I wonder what he's doing here?

2D He's up to no good, he is. Look! "He is suspected of having been involved in several recent shady deals ..."

6D They must all be up to something, planning something.

2D "... including the Clock Patience Swindle, and the ... Pontoon Bank Job."

6D What could it be? What could he be after here? What could they be arranging?

2D Another job?

6D But what? And what have Jack Smart and Myra to do with it? And with Q herself?

2D We'll ask Shiner.

6D Who?

2D Jack Flash! We'll ask him.

6D We can't ask him, he thinks we already know.

2D Oh!

6D We'll have to trick the information out of him — by pretending we know the plan.

2D How?

6D We'll have to be casual and careful and subtle.

2D Easy! Leave it to me!

6D He's coming back now.

Jack Flash enters

Jack Flash Not long now, a few minutes to half-time.

2D (*unsubtlely*) Tell us about the plan then!

Jack Flash What?

6D He says, "we're in on the plan then."

Jack Flash Good! Good! All organized is it?

2D Is it?

6D (*nudging 2D viciously*) Yes! Oh my word, yes. All organized, well and truly organized, by ... *you know who*.

Jack Flash Not arf!

2D Who?

6D (*nudging 2D*) A brilliant plan isn't it?

Jack Flash Brilliant! There's no other word for it.

2D But what is it?

6D (*nudging 2D*) It's a stroke of genius.

Jack Flash I'll say. I said to herself, I said, "with a plan like this, you don't have to worry", I said. There'll be lots in it for us all—plenty of the folding stuff, all round. Once we've got away with the whatsits they'll be none the wiser. We'll be away before you can say Jack Robinson. A plan and a half it is—beautiful. We'll all be in clover in no time at all. Once we have the stuff I can get the readies and then we are home and dry leaving the rest of them up the creek without a paddle. We'll be sitting there on a stack, absolutely alakeefick—it's an absolute piece of cake. Talk about having jam on it—I should cocoa—eh?

6D Oh . . . er . . . yes.

2D I couldn't have put it better myself.

Jack Flash So, see you later then. Usual place for the meeting tonight is it?

2D Usual place?

Jack Flash Thought so! See you there then! Take care of yourselves. Ciao!

Jack Flash exits

6D What usual place?

2D I don't understand. What was all that about? I tried to be casual and careful and subtle.

6D We ought to be there . . . at this meeting!

2D I didn't follow it. All that talk about cocoa and pieces of cake and jam on it—is it a party somewhere?

6D Where could it be?

2D It sounded good, didn't it? He said there'd be plenty of folding stuff—is that sandwiches?

6D What do you think?

2D I think there'll be sandwiches and plenty of this jam, cake and cocoa.

6D Cocoa?

2D At the party.

6D The meeting—where is it?

2D Where? I'll look in the paper.

6D We'll have to go you know.

2D I love parties. I don't go to many—I keep being left out.

6D It's going to be the only way of finding out the plan.

2D What about here! (*Reading the newspaper*) The Bridge Club.

6D Could that be it?

2D I've heard of that somewhere.

6D (*reading*) "Members Only!"

2D Quite recently someone said that . . .

6D That's a problem . . .

2D Someone in here . . . when I came back . . .

6D It could be them! That could be it! This might be the place! It's tonight!

2D The party?

6D And we'll be there too.

2D Is that "too" meaning "as well" or "two" meaning me?

6D Yes!

2D Ah! But I thought you said members only.

6D We'll get in somehow—we'll disguise ourselves. Come on!

6D exits

2D Coming! Disguise ourselves—oh yes I fancy that! Dressing up, eh! I could go as . . . as . . . a Three! What about that? . . . or . . . or what about as a five . . . or even . . . a seven? Oh yes, I fancy myself as a seven. What about that then—me—going to a party . . . as a seven! What does it say in the paper? "The Bridge Club-Entertainment for all!" That includes me. "Wine, dine and be entertained—every night!" I can hardly wait! "Members Only!" But I'll be in disguise! Ha! ha! Wait a minute, what's this in small print? "Non-members and uninvited guests will be sorry they tried to get in!"

Pause. 2D takes a long look at the audience

Sometimes I don't think I'm making the right decisions.

6D runs in and grabs 2D

6D Come on!

6D drags 2D offstage

2D (*as he goes*) No! No! I've changed my mind. Leave me out! I want you to leave me out! Are you listening?

CURTAIN

ACT II

Outside the Bridge Club that evening. The Club's interior is beyond

2D enters wearing an obviously false beard, a cloak and floppy hat

2D This is it, the entrance to the Bridge Club. I'm a bit early. (*To the audience*) It's me—could you tell? Ssh! Not a word, I'm in disguise. I won't be recognized dressed like this—clever, eh? I wonder where Six is? I don't like waiting around like this—I feel very conspic ... conscrip ... cons ... as though everybody's looking at me.

6D enters disguised as the Six of Spades

6D There you are. Sorry I'm late.

2D I don't know you ... go away. I don't know any Spades and *I'm* not a two anyway.

6D You know *me*. And you're the Two of Diamonds.

2D I'm not. I'm in disg ... I mean ... I ... go away. I'm waiting for a friend. And he's bigger than you—he's a six ...

6D It's *me* you fool. I'm a Six ...

2D Yes I can see that, you're a six, but you're a Spade. You're a Six of Spades ... and the person I'm waiting for is a six of ... something else's. Now go away.

6D I'm in disguise, aren't I? Remember?

2D In disguise? Wait a minute ... keep still—keep still! Good heavens ... yes it is *you*.

6D Of course it's me.

2D I didn't recognize you, did I. What a good disguise. I say, look, do you know who I am? (*He adjusts his beard*)

6D The Two of Diamonds.

2D Look carefully now. Can you tell—who am I?

6D The Two of Diamonds. How many more times? You should have got yourself a disguise.

2D What d'you mean? What about the beard and the hat and the cloak, eh? What about all that?

6D Yes, but what happens when we get inside?

2D We find out the plan and then give them what for! Fisticuffs all round! We'll take them and their plan to pieces ... won't you?

6D No, you fool, listen. When we get inside, they'll take our hats and coats. (*He removes 2D's hat and cloak*) And then ... we'll see you're a two of diamonds.

2D still wears his diamonds obviously

But *I'll* look like the Six of Spades still.
2D I'd never thought about that. What can we do?
6D Let me think?
2D Let's go home, eh? Perhaps it was a bad idea after all.
6D No. Wait a minute. We need to get inside to find out details of the plan.
Look, come here . . . I'll take some Spades off here (*He points to his shirt*)
and put them on you.

He takes two Spades from his front and puts them over 2D's diamonds

There. Now you're the Two of Spades and I'm the Four. What's the
matter?
2D Can't I be a three?
6D How?
2D Give us another spade!
6D Don't be silly. If I do that then we'll both be threes, won't we? What
would they say to that?
2D Snap?
6D Don't be foolish. Come on. You don't need the beard.
2D I feel safer in it.
6D I'll knock at the door. (*He knocks at the door*)
2D I'm scared. Are you sure they'll let us in?
6D Leave it to me . . . and don't panic!

The door opens: Jackson looks out

Ah, good evening; my friend and I, both members of this particular
establish . . .
Jackson Thank goodness. Come on in, what kept you?
6D Pardon?
Jackson They're all waiting for you—come on!
6D No, you don't understand—it's us. And we appear to have left our
membership cards in our other suits, so . . .
2D They're diamonds actually . . . our other sui . . .
6D Quiet! Leave it to me!
Jackson Come on. Don't hang around here.
6D What?
Jackson She's inside. Come on . . . quickly—don't keep her waiting.
2D Ah, yes but you don't . . .
Jackson No buts. You're both needed . . . come on!
2D Can't I wait outside? Please?
Jackson Not likely. You're wanted—inside! Now!

2D and 6D are moved towards the inside of the Club

2D Just a moment. There's something you ought to know.
6D Quiet, you fool. Things are working out better than I thought.

Inside: A bar at rear. Jack Smart and Myra at a table, waited on by 3D

Jack Smart Blimey Myra, I don't 'arf feel out of me depth here.

Myra Oh, for heaven's sake Jack, how can we ever get into the big time with you acting scared like that? Where's your confidence?

Jack Smart But I've never been here before, have I. I mean.

Myra Get used to it, Jack. From now on we'll be able to afford places like this.

Jack Smart Yeah—that's right. I never thought of it that way. You're right.

3D Would you care for a drink, sir?

Jack Smart What? Oh yes. Oh my word, yes ... what'll it be Myra?

Myra Er ... I'll have the same as you Jack.

Jack Smart Oh yeah. Well, in that case ... two ... two ... two ...

Myra What do you recommend?

3D Most customers enjoy the Bridge Club Specials.

Jack Smart Yeah—that's right. Two of them.

Myra And make it quick!

Jack Smart Don't mix it, Myra!

3D moves to the bar and gets drinks

Q enters

Q Ah. There you are. Sorry to keep you waiting.

Jack Smart Not at all. Don't mention it.

Q It's just that I'm expecting two of my "colleagues" to arrive. The ones I entrust with my "special" jobs ... you know what I mean?

Jack Smart Do we?

Myra Of course, of course Q. *We* understand.

Q I've got Jackson at the door keeping a look out for them. As soon as they arrive he'll let us know. I want them in on the plan. We'll need them.

Jack Smart Of course we will.

Myra We don't want no violence.

Q Of course we don't. But we need to be prepared, don't we. Now ... what about the details of the plan?

The Queen of Hearts (QH) enters, preceded by the Four of Diamonds (4D)

4D *(announcing)* Her Majesty the Queen of Hearts!

Q Oh good lord—what's she doing here?

Jack Smart Well, as we see it ... this is the plan ...

Q Quiet! Not now you fool—later.

QH Good evening, ladies and gentlemen. How pleasant to see you all here this evening. I was only saying to my husband, the ... the ... the ...

4D *(whispering to QH)* The King.

QH ... the other day that no where else in the world can one find as many loyal and pleasant-looking subjects as ... as ... as ...

4D *(whispering to QH)* As here.

QH As a matter of fact that is why I am with you all to ... to ... to ...

4D *(whispering to QH)* ... tonight!

QH ... to encourage you all to enter my wonderful nationwide cookery competition to be held ... next ... next ... next ...

4D *(whispering to QH)* ... week!

QH ... next door to the Central Stadium on the very day of the Cup Final that will decide the winners of the magnificent ... magnificent ... magnificent ...

4D (*whispering to QH*) Trophies!

QH ... seven cups and the gold medals. But at the same time there will be my Cookery Competition and we have details ... details ... details ...

4D (*whispering to QH*) Here!

QH ... of how to enter. Just give them out, will you?

4D and 3D give out leaflets

Q Come on, let's find somewhere quiet to talk.

Jack Smart But what about our plan?

Q What do you think we'll be talking about stupid? Come on!

Myra But we haven't had our drinks yet!

Jack Smart Don't mix it, Myra. Come on!

   Q, Jack Smart and Myra exit one side of the stage

   6D and 2D and Jackson enter the other side of the stage

QH moves to another table

Jackson Come on, you two. You take your time don't you?

2D (*to 6D*) What'll we do?

6D Don't panic. Leave it all to me.

Jackson Now then. Where's she gone?

2D Perhaps she changed her mind? Perhaps it's all off. Perhaps we can go home? Perhaps ...

6D Quiet! Perhaps you'll give the game away.

Jackson You'd better sit down and wait. I'll go and get them.

6D Right.

Jackson Sit here. (*Indicating the table that Q has left*)

6D Thank you.

Jackson (*to 2D*) And you!

2D Thanks! (*He sits reluctantly*)

QH (*shouting across*) I say, you there. You two.

2D Pardon?

QH I said you two.

2D Me?

QH Both of you two!

2D No, he's the six. I'm the two.

6D (*loud whisper*) I'm a four.

2D Oops sorry! Yes, he's a four, I'm the two ... of *Spades*.

QH Have you got the ... the ... the ...

2D Time?

QH ... form for the cookery ... cookery ... cookery ...

6D Book?

QH ... competition. You *will* have a ... a ... a ...

2D Drink?

QH ... go, won't you?

6D Go, where?
QH There's an absolutely super . . . super . . . super . . .
2D Man?
QH . . . prize for the winner. Make sure you have your entry forms. The winner could be . . . could be . . . could be . . .

4D hands across two entry forms

2D You.
QH No, not me silly! I can't enter the competition.
2D What a pity!
QH Isn't it. I was only saying the other day to my . . . my . . .
2D Self?
QH . . . husband; "What a pity, Reginald", I said, "that I can't comp . . . comp . . . comp . . ."
6D Compete.
QH . . . comprehend a way of entering some of my own baking and he said . . .
2D Do it!
QH Pardon?
2D I said, "do it", your highness, you enter some tarts. Show 'em how it's done.
QH But the rules?
6D Enter them in *our* name, your higheness.
QH The Two and Four of Spades.
2D Yes! No!
QH No?
6D Just in case anyone might have seen us talking together. Why not call us the . . .
2D . . . Two and Six of Diamonds.
QH What a good . . . good . . . good . . .
6D Idea.
QH Bye! I'll go and see to it right . . . right . . . right . . .
2D Away?
QH . . . turn. And off we go. Come along!

QH sweeps out, followed by 4D

6D What a funny . . . funny . . . funny . . .
2D Thing?
6D Woman. Now come on, let's not waste any more time.

They sit. 3D moves from the bar

3D The drinks that were ordered, sir.

3D exits

2D What?
6D Thank you.
2D I didn't order any.
6D Shut up. Drink it. Look natural. There's someone coming.

Jack Flash, 10C and 2S enter

Jack Flash Over here boys. Take a seat. I'll just get us a drink or two

They sit at a table. Jack Flash goes to the bar

2D (*drinking*) It's very powerful stuff. (*He splutters*)
6D What's the matter?

2D points to his drink

Drink it slowly.
Jack Flash Here we are lads. Just the thing. This'll see you all right. Here's mud in your eye.
10C Cheers!
2S All the best!

2D, 2S, 10C, Jack Flash and 6D drink. There is no effect

6D What's the matter now?
2D (*sounding strangled*) I think I've lost my voice!
6D Don't say such things. And stop drawing attention to yourself. Try to look casual.

2D attempts to look casual

Jack Flash How does that grab you, boys. Just the cat's pyjamas, eh?
10C Very good, Shiner.
2S Very good indeed.
10C Now what's the game?
Jack Flash I'll explain. It's a big one. Lots of the readies all round—and I mean the green and crinkly stuff.
10C I'll drink to that.
2S Me too!

10C and 2S drink

6D Now listen carefully—are you listening?

2D nods furiously

We already know there's something big planned, don't we.

2D nods furiously

But we don't know what it is.

2D shakes his head equally furiously

So we keep our eyes and ears open.

2D mimes keeping eyes and ears open

Then we can make *our* plans to stop *their* plans.

2D nods furiously

3D approaches their table

3D Can I get you anything else, sir?
2D I'll have the same again!
6D What!
2D Sssh!

3D returns to the bar for the order

10C Nice place this, Shiner!
2S Very nice indeed!
Jack Flash Stick with me, boys, and dives like this will be just the beginning.
   Together we'll really go places. Ready for another?

10C and 2S nod. 3D brings 2D a drink

Jack Flash (*shouting*) Another round over here, miss. Quick as you can.

3D goes to take the order from Jack Flash, and returns to the bar

2D Oh heck. Look at that. D'you see who it is?
6D Where?
2D Sitting over there. It's Jack Flash—Shiner ... you know, that bloke we
   were talking to. Now we're in trouble.
6D No, we're not. We're in disguise, aren't we. He'll never recognize us.
   We're Spades now.
2D Phew! Thank heavens. I thought we'd be found out. (*He takes a copious
   drink and splutters appropriately*)
6D Oh dear. Oh my word. Oh great heavens!
2D It's all right! I'm all right! You don't have to worry about me! I'll be all
   right! I said I'll be all right!
6D Ssh! Quiet! We do have a problem.
2D What's that?
6D Don't look now.

2D half-turns

   I said *don't* look ... but sitting over there is the Two of Spades.
2D Really? I don't know him. Do you?
6D The ... Two ... of ... Spades. (*He indicates 2D's disguise*)
2D Oh, the Two of Spades. *That* ... Two ... of ... Sp ... What? But I'm
   the ... Oh dear. What're we going to do?
6D Don't panic. Keep cool. Have a drink.

*2D drinks but chokes spectacularly, stands up and in doing so draws the
attention of the other table*

10C Look at that!
2S Blimey!
Jack Flash Well, well. What have we here? An imposter!
2S He's impostering me!
10C You're not the Two of Spades!
2S No, you're not. *I* am.
Jack Flash What've you got to say to that?

2D coughs and splutters further and 6D bangs him on the back

6D He's not feeling well.

10C I'll give him "not feeling well". Just let me get my hands on 'im.

Jack Flash Wait a minute, 'aven't I seen you somewhere before?

6D and 2D shake there heads furiously

Are you quite sure?

6D and 2D nod furiously

10C Let's fill 'em in now, Flash. Ask questions afterwards.

2S Sort 'em out, Shiner. That's what they need.

Jack Flash In a minute. In a minute. Just let me think.

6D We can explain if you'll let us.

Jack Flash Go on then! We're all ears.

Pause

QH and 4D enter

QH Done! Done! All done just as you suggested. What a good idea. I wish I'd thought of it. Marvellous, marvellous. I've got my cook working on them now . . . just wait until you see my . . . my . . . my . . .

4D Entry!

QH . . . tarts. Or rather *your* tarts, you clever little people you. You're quite the cleverest pair of . . . of . . . of . . .

2D ⎱ Spades!
6D ⎰

QH . . . Diamonds I've ever met in all my . . . my . . . my . . .

4D Life!

QH Goodness is that the time? Come along, can't wait around here any longer. There are things to . . . to . . . to . . .

4D Do!

QH Come along! Come along!

QH and 4D exit

Jack Flash *Diamonds!* I thought as much. You're the two I met this afternoon. You were the two at the match weren't you?

2D Was I?

Jack Flash I recognize you now.

6D Do you?

10C Can we fill 'em in now then, Shiner?

2S Flippin' imposters. Let's give 'em what for.

6D Run!

6D and 2D run through the audience

10C Come on . . . let's get after them!

10C and 2S chase them through the audience

Jack Flash Wait a minute! They're on *our* side—I think! Hang on a minute, lads.

The chase continues—out of the auditorium possibly

   Q, Jack Smart and Myra enter with Jackson

Q Shiner! Where have you been? We've been waiting for you.

Jack Flash What? Oh, sorry Q. It's just that . . .

Q Just nothing. Now let's get all this plan sorted out. It's all taken too long already.

Jack Smart Right.

Myra Right. I should say so . . . keeping us hanging around like this.

Jack Smart (*whispering*) Don't mix it, Myra!

Q Are you with us, Shiner? What's the matter with you?

Jack Flash Nothing, Q. Nothin'—it's all in hand.

Q What is?

Jack Flash My lads are just dealing with a couple of . . . non-members. Two of your blokes, Smartie, pretending to be Spades.

Jack Smart My blokes?

Myra Who can that be, Jack?

Q Have you been talking, Jack?

Jack Smart Nothin' to do with me. Who d'you mean?

Jack Flash I remember—it's the Six and Two of Diamonds!

Myra Oh no! Not him again!

Jackson I should have finished 'im off before, Boss, when I had time.

Q Quiet Jackson!

Jack Smart But what're they doing here?

Jack Flash You mean they're not some of your lads?

Jack Smart You must be joking!

Jack Flash Well, not to worry, me old sunshine, 'cos *my* lads'll soon catch up with them.

Q You're sure?

Jack Flash The Ten of Blackberries'll sort 'em out right enough. They'll wish they'd never tried it on with us. Don't you worry your pretty little . . .

Jackson Shall I go after 'em, Boss?

Q Cool it, Jackson! If Shiner says everything is in hand then it is! Let's get on with the real business.

Jack Smart Ready when you are.

Myra And not before time.

Q
Jack Smart } (*together*) Don't mix it Myra!

They all group and sit round a table and conspire with 3D watching behind the bar

   During the next 6D and 2D enter behind the conspirators very tentatively, bump into each other, jump, signal each other to keep quiet and are waved into hiding behind the bar by 3D

Q Who's going to begin? Jack?

Jack Smart Well, it's like this. As you know, Q, we—that is Myra here and myself have, for a long time, been considering the possibility—only the possibility mind you—of . . .

Q Get to the point. We've wasted enough time as it is.

Jack Smart Quite. I do agree, and therefore . . .

Jack Flash What's the caper?

Jack Smart Pardon?

Jack Flash What's the game? The plan? Blimey, don't you even understand plain English?

Jack Smart I'll tell you if you'll just listen . . .

Myra What we aim to do is to take advantage at the Cup Final next week of . . .

Jack Smart Pinching all the trophies and the gold medals.

Myra And the gate receipts—all the ticket money and making ourselves very scarce.

Jack Smart Going where no one will ever find us.

6D, 2D and 3D are open-mouthed

2D sneezes, 6D, 2D and 3D all duck below the bar

During the next the characters below turn to Jackson and speak together

Jack Smart ⎫
Q ⎬ Bless you.
Myra ⎭
Jack Flash Gesundheit.

10C and 2S enter looking around

Q Wait a minute though. All those trophies and medals are likely to be won by *my* team.

Jackson You tell 'em, boss.

Q So why do I want to pinch them?

Jack Smart Why? Why? Because . . . *you* explain Myra.

Myra Because this way they become yours *for ever*—you don't have to give them back.

10C and 2S search around the stage; 6D, 2D and 3D behind the bar slowly emerge above the bar level. 10C and 2S go out into audience searching

Jack Flash Any luck yet boys?

10C Still looking for 'em, Shiner.

2S We'll get 'em, don't worry!

Jack Smart And not only that, Q—we'll have the takings as well . . . to share.

Myra Fifty-fifty.

Jack Smart What d'you say?

2D sneezes; 6D, 2D and 3D duck down below the bar

During the next the characters below turn to Jackson, speaking simultaneously

Jack Smart ⎫
10C   ⎪
Q   ⎬ (*together*) Bless you.
2S   ⎪
Myra   ⎭
Jack Flash Gesundheit.
Q I like it!
Jack Flash And where do I come into it?
Jack Smart Where?
Jack Flash What's in it for me?
Q Well, it's obvious isn't it, Jack? We'll need you to get rid of the trophies
and the medals for us—to find a customer or to get the stuff melted down.

10C and 2S continue searching

Myra That's right!
Jack Flash So it's a three-way split.
Q Yes.
Jack Smart Yes.
Myra No!
Q
Jack Smart (*together*) Don't mix it Myra!
Myra Jack—we said fifty-fifty.
Jack Smart That was before . . .
Myra So what's different now?
Jack Flash I am, my darlin'. And there's my assistants to be paid too.
Myra I still think the split's wrong. After all, it was our idea . . . and . . .
Q   ⎫
Jack Smart ⎪
Jack Flash ⎬ (*together*) Don't mix it Myra!
Jackson   ⎪
10C   ⎪
2S   ⎭
Myra . . . Oh, all right I agree.

2D sneezes and 6D, 2D and 3D duck below the bar

Jack Smart ⎫
Jackson   ⎪
Q   ⎬ (*together*) Bless you.
Myra   ⎭
Jack Flash Gesundheit.

Jack Smart, Jack Flash, Q and Myra realize Jackson spoke too

Jack Flash Hang about. We are not alone.
Jack Smart What d'you mean?
Myra Who else is here?
Q Jackson!

Jackson looks round

Jack Flash There's somebody else in here besides us four!

10C There's us down here, Shiner.

Jack Flash Someone else other than you I mean. Come back 'ere, the pair of you.

Jack Smart Who can it be?

Myra Where can they be?

Q Keep quite! Listen! All of you.

Pause. A sneeze from behind the bar

Jackson
Jack Smart ⎫
Q ⎬ *(together)* Bless you.
Myra ⎭

Jack Flash Gesundheit.

Q Right then! Come on out! We know you're there.

Pause

Don't make it difficult for yourself—come on out now.

Pause

I don't want to have to use force but I will if you make me. Are you ready Jackson?

Jackson More than ready, Boss!

Jack Flash Come on—out of it! Or you'll regret it. The lads 'ere'll knock spots off you. Are you listenin'?

Q I shall count up to five and then we're coming for you. One ... two ... three ... four ...

3D emerges with her hands up

3D Don't shoot! Don't shoot! I'm coming out!

Q Who said anything about shooting? Come here.

3D comes out from behind the bar

And sit down!

3D sits or is forcibly sat down

Q Now then. Three isn't it?

3D Of Diamonds.

Q What were you doing behind there?

3D Er ... washing up?

Jack Flash All the time?

3D That's right.

Q You weren't listening by any chance?

3D No. I mean. What to? I don't know what you mean.

Myra You're not so simple. Let me get my hands on her, Q, I'll soon find out the truth.

Jack Smart Stay out of it, Myra!

Q Jack's right—we'll handle this little ... problem. Jackson!

Jackson Yes boss?
Q Just find out if this little Diamond is telling us the truth.
Jackson With pleasure, Boss. Just give me a hand, you lads.
10C Righto!
2S Any time!
Jackson Stand back the rest of you while we get at the truth.
3D What do you mean?

Jackson, 10C and 2S roll up their sleeves

What are you going to do?

Jackson, 10C and 2S close in on her

I don't know anything. I didn't hear anything ... honest!
Q I'll give you one more chance. What were you really doing behind that bar?

Pause

All right Jackson, she's all yours!

But as Jackson approaches 3D menacingly a crash comes from behind the bar and draws the attention of all on stage. Pause. 2D and 6D emerge slowly from behind the Bar dressed as jokers—they come out from each end of the bar. 6D is confident, 2D is petrified

6D Good evening ladies and gentlemen. And welcome to the Bridge Club this evening. We are here to entertain you, and you, and you. So take a seat, sit back and enjoy yourselves.

And surprisingly they do, becoming an audience for 6D and 2D

2D (*sotto voce*) What are you doing?
6D (*sotto voce*) We're going to entertain them?
2D (*sotto voce*) We are?
6D (*sotto voce*) That's right.
2D (*sotto voce*) How?
6D (*sotto voce*) Just follow by example.

During the next 6D "reads" the jokes from inside his cuff, sleeves, lapels, etc. 2D soon catches on where the jokes are to be found—and becomes over-confident leading to his not being able to find the right reply for the last joke. The joke sequence is as follows—but could be extended or shortened according to performance

(*To audience*) Good evening. How nice to see you.
2D Thank you very much.
6D (*sotto voce*) Not *you*, you fool, them.
2D Oh!
6D But while you're here; (*Looking under his cuff*) what's yellow on the inside and green on the outside?
2D (*sotto voce*) What're you talking about?

6D (*pointedly looking under his cuff*) What's yellow on the inside and green on the outside?

2D (*catching on and looking under his cuff*) A banana disguised as a cucumber?

6D I say, if you breathe oxygen during the day, what do you breathe at night?

2D Nitrogen!

6D Don't be silly. I wish you would pay a little attention!

2D I'm paying as little as I can!

6D What's a crocodile's favourite card game?

2D Snap!

6D What's the best birthday present?

2D Well, a drum takes a bit of beating.

6D Doctor! Doctor! I feel like a pack of cards.

2D Sit down and I'll *deal* with you later.

6D Doctor! Doctor! I keep thinking I'm invisible.

2D Go shopping. The change will do you good!

6D I said—I keep thinking I'm invisible.

2D Sorry! Sit down I'll *deal* with you later!

6D Get it right! I keep thinking I'm invisible.

2D Well a drum takes a bit of beating.

6D (*sotto voce*) What're you doing?

2D (*sotto voce*) I can't find the answer!

6D (*sotto voce*) Look for it! Look for it! Doctor! Doctor! I keep thinking I'm invisible.

2D Just a minute! (*Taking off his coat*) Ah! Who said that?

But now, of course, we can see who he really is

2S It's 'im!

10C It's them!

Jackson Look boss!

Q Get them!

A chase ensues on and off stage: ad lib.

2D I wish *I* was invisible!

CURTAIN

ACT III

Behind the scenes/dressing area of the sports stadium. A week later

It is the day of the Grand Final

*6D and 2D are still disguised as the Four of Spades and the Two of Spades.
With 3D, they are bundled in by 10C and 2S; they are tied and blindfolded*

2D Leave me alone, you bully! Let me go! Let me go! You've no right to
treat us like this! Who do you think you are? I'm a law-abiding criticism I
am.

6D Citizen!

2D Yes, that as well! You've kept us prisoner for at least a week. And I
don't like it! So you can leave me out . . . please! I don't want any part of
this deal. I pay my . . .

2S Shut up! Will yer . . . or I'll fill you in.

2D Oh, that's nice; that's nice, isn't it—fill *me* in.

2S Any time you like. I've had just about enough of you this last week.

2D You've had enough of *me*? Enough of *me*?

6D Oh, do be quiet, the pair of you. Give us all the time to think.

2D I've had time to think. We've *all* had time to think. I want to get out of
here.

3D Don't we all.

10C And you can keep quiet an' all. You're in enough trouble as it is,
involved with these two.

3D But I was only washing up.

10C That's what they all say.

6D She's right, though, she's not with us.

2S Well she is *now*!

10C She's involved enough now!

Q and Jackson enter

Q No sign of the others yet?

2S Who's that then?

Q Jack Smart and that Myra.

10C We ain't seen 'em, Boss.

2D Excuse me. But I wonder if I might have a word with you?

Q Shut 'em up, Jackson—and sit 'em down!

Jackson Sure thing Boss. Come on now, you three. Put a sock in it, will ya!

2D, 6D and 3D are sat down by the others

2D Careful with me! Careful, I'm fragrant.

Jackson Fragrant? I thought I could smell something.

6D He means fragile.

2S I'll "fragile" 'im—impostering me! I'll give 'im what for.

3D What for?

2S For pretending to be *me*, that's what for!

Jackson Leave it out, will ya! There'll be time for all that later.

3D I was afraid of that.

Jack Flash enters

Jack Flash Come on, Q. We can't 'ang about much longer. The game's almost about to start. They've made the cut and both hands are ready. So what about the job? Who's doing what? And when do we start?

Q We need Jack Smart and that pushy side-kick of his—they've got the details.

Jack Flash Well, where are they?

Q I don't know where they are. I thought they'd be here by now.

6D I wouldn't trust 'em an inch if I were you.

10C Shut up you!

6D Well, don't say you weren't warned.

10C Did you hear me?

6D All right! All right! I'll say no more.

Pause

Jack Flash He could be right Q. 'Ere we are waiting for those two . . . and they could have sloped off you know . . .

6D They might even have done the job already.

Jack Flash What?

6D Without you!

Q Come on. Let's go and look for 'em. Come on. You as well, Jackson.

Q and Jack Flash exit

10C What about us?

Jackson Keep your eye on these three.

2S Yes, but . . .

Jackson Do as you're told. We'll be back!

10C Oh, that's bloomin' great, that is!

2S What d'you mean, Ten?

10C Leavin' us 'ere to look after these three.

2S Baby-minding is it?

2D Who are you calling a baby?

2S (*threateningly*) Who do *you* think?

2D I was only asking. Goo . . . goo (*He makes baby noises*)

10C *We're* supposed to be the heavy mob.

2S Yeah.

10C That's what Shiner said. We'll need *you*, 'e said, for when the going gets rough.

2S When the going gets rough?

10C The rough get going.

6D That's you, right enough.

10C What do you mean?

6D You're the rough ones ... the ones they'll be relying on.

10C That's right!

2S Not 'arf!

6D You ought to be out there with 'em now.

10C Now?

6D In case they need you.

3D In case there's trouble.

2D In case there's a fight.

10C You're right.

2S Not 'arf!

6D You could leave us here.

3D We can't get up to anything.

2D After all we're tied up.

6D And blindfolded.

10C Your *right* again.

2S Not 'arf again.

6D So what are you waiting for?

3D They need you out there.

2D We'll be all right—don't worry about us! We'll manage somehow. We'll miss you of course but then all good things must come to an end sometime. It's the way of the worm.

6D World!

2D Is it? So don't let us keep you.

10C 'Ere, you're not trying to get rid of us are you?

6D Of course not.

3D My word, no.

2D Whatever gave you that idea.

10C Right then. Come on, they may need a hand.

2S Not 'arf. Coming.

10C and 2S exit

2S returns

You'll be all right won't you?

6D ⎫		Certainly.
2D ⎬	*(together, ad. lib)*	Don't worry about us.
3D ⎭		'Course we will.

2S exits

3D and 2D immediately get up and walk about, hesitatingly, since they are still blindfolded

6D Phew! That was close. I thought they'd never go.

3D It was very clever of you.

2D Thank you!

3D Not you—him!

6D You mean me.

3D That's right. Where are you?

6D Here! Where are you?
2D I'm here. Where are you?
3D You mean me?
6D Not you. Two, her—Three.
3D I'm here.
2D Why not me, Six? Why her?
6D 'Cos I'm talking to her.
2D Aren't you talking to me anymore?
6D Of course I am.
2D You've not fallen out with me then?
6D Of course I haven't. Now stop being foolish.
3D Are you talking to me?
6D No, I'm not talking to you.
3D Why, what have I done?

The next to be spoken in unison

6D No . . . you don't understand. When I said "I'm not talking to you", I didn't mean I wasn't talking to *you*. I meant I wasn't at that particular moment talking directly to you—or rather directing my conversation towards you. (etc.)
3D I mean I know I haven't known you all that long, but I thought we at least trusted each other and could talk together—discuss mutual problems you know, rather than end up arguing as though we'd known each other years. (etc.)
2D If you've fallen out with me, you've only got to say so, I won't be upset, I won't mind . . . well not all that much anyway. I mean I can take a hint you know. I'm not insensible you know, I have my feelings too. If you've had enough of my friendship all you have to do is say so . . . I don't mind. (etc.)
6D Stop! Hold everything! Quiet you two.

3D carries on talking ad lib

. . . and you, Three! Now listen. We're going to get nowhere until we get rid of these blindfolds. Now listen. If you come to me, and we stand back to back we can untie our hands, and then we can remove our blindfolds—right?
3D } *(together)* Right!
2D } Yes—I get you!
6D So, let's do it . . . now!

2D, 3D and 6D move, calling instructions to each other, etc. 2D will obviously be on the wrong end of everything and might comment accordingly, saying, "watch out", "don't do that—it tickles", "ooh! be careful what you're doing". They free each other

QH enters with 4D and 5D in attendance. They carry a table between them set with a cloth

QH We'll just have to set it up here, then. If they can't be bothered to open the hall on time, then we'll have the judging done in . . . in . . . in . . .

4D Here?

QH ... no time at all. (*To 3D, 2D and 6D*) And you judges can make your decisions. Oh splendid, splendid—yes I like the blindfolds. What a super idea so that you won't be able to ... to ... to ...

5D See?

QH ... cheat in any way at all. What a perfectly wizard idea. I wish I'd thought of it. No, no; don't take them off, let's just see how you'll look. Mm ... yes, oh my word yes. It looks right, just ... just ... just ...

4D The job?

QH ... a moment. Now is there anything I've forgotten? We've got the table now, and the judges, so all we need is the ... the ... the ...

5D Tarts?

QH ... will to win! What a splendid achievement! What a spectacular occasion! Wait until my husband sees all that I've done in his ... his ... his ...

4D Absence?

QH ... name. How proud he'll be. There now, let's go and see to the rest of it. The entries should be arriving any time now and we don't want to be ... to be ... to be ...

4D ⎫ Or not to be.
5D ⎭

QH That's the question! Come along you two.

2D attempts to move but 6D and 3D restrain him

Let's put our best foot ... foot ... foot ...

4D In it?

5D On it?

4D To it?

5D With it?

QH Forward!

4D, 5D and QH exit

6D, 3D and 2D take off their blindfolds

6D I thought she'd never go.

3D Doesn't she talk a lot? You can't get a word in sideways!

2D Ah ha! So *this* is where we are—I recognize this place. Now who'd have thought it? Did you realize, Six?

6D Of course I did. Where else could we be. The Grand Final has started and those crooks'll be about to pinch the trophies.

3D The gold medals.

2D And the ticket money.

6D And we've got to stop them.

3D How?

Pause

6D Look out. There's someone coming. Quick, hide.

2D, 3D and 6D look round

3D (*indicating the table cloth*) Under here.

6D, 3D and 2D hide under the table set up for the tart-judging

Q, Jack Smart, Jack Flash, Myra and Jackson enter

Q I thought we'd never find you. There's quite a crowd up there!
Jack Smart It is rather full.
Jack Flash Full? Blimey, that's an understatement. You couldn't cram any more in—not even with a shoe-horn and a jar of lubricating oil.
Myra What a beautiful turn of phrase you do have.
Jack Flash I always knew you fancied me, sweetheart.
Q Quiet Shiner! There's work to be done.
Jackson Hey Boss! Boss!
Q Not now Jackson.
Jackson Yes, but Boss ...
Q I said "*not now Jackson*".

Jackson is concerned as to where the guards and prisoners have gone

So, let's have the details of the plan. And let's have them quickly; we all need to be seen around up there so that no suspicion can fall on us until we're hundreds of miles away.
Jack Flash You're right, Boss!
Q So come on. How's it done?

3D, 2D and 6D look out from their hiding place. Since Jackson is looking round this has to be done with care

Jack Smart Well ... I've given ...

Myra nudges Jack Smart

Sorry. *We've* given it plenty of thought and it's like this ...
Jack Flash Come on! Come on!
Q Make it fast!
Myra Oh, let me explain. First, Q. You'll be on the platform, so you take the trophies—all seven, one at a time and pass them to you, Shiner ... you pass them to me and I pass them to Jack who brings them down here and puts them in the boxes we have hidden in the cupboard at the back there.

This coincides with Jackson, on his search opening the appropriate cupboard and the boxes falling on him

Those are the ones. Then we do the same with the gold medals, putting them in one box. After that Shiner and I go and collect the takings from the turnstiles, put it all in two bags, and again give it to Jack to put in boxes. Eight boxes in all. After the interval we all carry out the boxes to our get-away car ... and we're off. Is that clear?

The conspirators and the eavesdroppers all nod

So let's go to it!
Jackson Wait! Stop! All of you!

Q What's the matter now, Jackson?

Could the eavesdroppers have been seen?

Jack Flash What's the grumble?
Myra Well?
Jack Smart What is it?
Jackson Where's the prisoners? And where's the ten of blackberries and the two of diggers that was with them?
Q Oh good lord. We haven't time for that now. You find them Jackson, you find them. Come on the rest of you!
Jack Flash There's no time to waste. The game's already started.
Jack Smart Come on Myra!
Myra But shouldn't we *find* them first, Jack?
Jack Smart How many times must we tell you?

Q
Jack Flash } (*together*) Don't mix it Myra!
Jack Smart

   Myra, Q, Jack Flash and Jack Smart exit

Jackson Wait a minute! I can't find 'em on me own. (*Pause*) They could be anywhere. I'd better look 'round here.

He begins to search; as he looks around the table area, peering under one end of the table, the trio of heroes come out of the other end

   They couldn't have gone far. Here's a blindfold, and another ... and here's some of the rope they were tied up with. They can't be all that far away.

6D
2D } (*miming*) What shall we do?
3D
6D (*miming to 3D*) Get Jackson's attention—I'll throw a tablecloth over him. (*To 2D*) Hit him.
3D (*miming*) What with?
6D (*miming*) I don't know.

2D goes to the stage's rear, opens a cupboard marked "Clubs" and takes out a large club

All this happens as they are still hidden from Jackson's searching

Jackson I shouldn't be doing this anyway. What's the point of getting some of the heavy boys in to do the nasty business and then having to do most of it yourself? I'm going to get out of this line of business after this lot, I'll get myself into a nice little gambling business somewhere—I'll go to Las Vegas or Monte Carlo. Go and work in a Casino. There's people always on the look out for good cards there, so they tell me ... (*He sees 3D*) ... hey, there you are. I've been looking for you.

Jackson approaches 3D but is caught by 2D, 6D, and 3D

2D It worked! It worked! We've got 'im!

6D Put him in the cupboard.

2D Which one?

6D Any one.

2D Give me a hand, Three.

They lift Jackson to the rear of the stage and open a cupboard. Boxes fall out

Oops! Let's just move these.

The boxes are moved and the unconscious Jackson put in the cupboard

6D Put the cloth back on the table. And the boxes.

2D and 3D do this

2D Easy! Easy! Easy! Let 'em all come, I say. We can take 'em, we can shake 'em. We can.

3D Only the Ten of Clubs and the Four of Spades to get now.

2D Who?

6D You heard her. There's the Ten of Clubs and the Four of Spades.

2D The Ten of Clubs, the ten of blackberries himself? Oh no! Not him! I met him once before: he was on the other side in that match I was playing—you remember. I don't want anything to do with him. He's viscous, he is.

6D Vicious!

2D A right sticky character he is. He trumped almost all our side. He's very rough. He's a Crimplene.

3D A criminal.

2D That as well. So come on. Let's go before he arrives. Let's get out while the going is good. Let's make a run for it now while we can. Let's go home and have a cup of tea.

During this speech 2D backs away from 6D and 3D, unaware that:

10C enters

2D backs right up against 10C

Come on, let's go. There's nothing to be gained by waiting around he ... (*He realizes*) Help!

10C chases 2D round the table

10C Come on, we've got him.

2D (*shouting*) Call him off, don't let him catch me! Don't just stand there— do something.

The chase can go through the front of the audience

Eventually 2D creeps under the table and 10C follows him. As 2D emerges at the other side. 3D and 6D "club" 10C as he emerges

6D Get him in the cupboard.

2D and 3D do this

2D You were a bit slow there. He might have caught me! Good job I have a good turn of speed! Fast . . . that's me. I could have been in our Olympic team you know. Have I ever mentioned that before?

2S enters

2S Ah, there you are! Now this is when I get my own back! All three of you, eh? Well I'll get you all then. Come 'ere, let me finish you off!

2S chases 2D, 3D and 6D

2D Help! I'm getting too old for this.
3D What about your Olympic experience?
6D Save your arguments till later!

2S catches 2D

2S I've got him! I've got him!

6D bends down behind 2S and 2D pushes 2S over 6D. 3D finishes the job off with a well-aimed "club". They all shake hands

6D Put him with the others.

3D and 2D do: ad. lib. about the fact that this is the third time they've had to do it!

Jack Smart enters handing a trophy to 6D

Jack Smart Here's the first, put it in a box. I'll be back with the others.

Jack Smart exits

2D Did you see that?
3D He just gave it to you?
6D So he did. And you know why?
2D Because you've won first prize?
6D No, you dope. Because he thinks I'm on his side. Look, you and I are still Spades as far as anyone can see—right?
2D Right!
6D So all we have to do is wait for the others.

Jack Smart enters

Jack Smart Here's two more: put 'em in boxes.

Jack Smart exits

2D Just like that.
3D I'll put 'em in the boxes. (*And she does*)
6D What did I tell you? Easy, isn't it?
2D This is the bit I like. The other running around bit was like hard work.
3D What? Even for an Olympic athlete like yourself?
2D Ah well. Perhaps I exaggerated just a little bit.
3D Perhaps you did.

Jack Smart enters

Jack Smart (*to 2D*) Here's some more. The plan's going like a dream. Any problems at this end?

2D None at all. It's going like a bomb.

Jack Smart No trouble with the prisoners?

2D Don't worry. *We've* dealt with it.

Jack Smart exits

3D boxes the trophies

6D That was a bit close.

2D No way! I was in command. He suspected nothing.

6D Don't be too sure.

2D Don't worry. I can handle it. Leave it to me. I'm in charge!

3D That's what we're afraid of.

Jack Smart enters again with more trophies and medals, via 6D, to 3D, and to the boxes

Jack Smart Here we are. The last lot. There's only the takings to come. Then we're home and dry, as Shiner would say. Phew! I could do with a rest.

6D Later, later. There's time for that later. Just finish getting the stuff.

2D No. Have a rest if you want. Take the weight off your feet. You've had a hard day.

Jack Smart Yes, I think I could do with a sit down. I'll just . . .

6D What would Q say?

Jack Smart (*jumping*) What? Oh yeah! You're right. Anyway just one more load and we're there. Won't be long!

Jack Smart exits

6D (*to 2D*) Fool! You nearly messed it up, then.

2D What do you mean? I thought I did that well. Cool I was, really cool!

6D A damn sight too cool. What do we do when the last lot arrives?

2D Good Lord, haven't you been taking notice? We put it in the boxes. Two loads of takings money, two boxes . . . one in each. Really, I would have thought it was easy enough to understand, you don't have to be a master piece.

6D Mind!

2D Of course I mind. What do you think?

3D No, listen. He means what happens then. When all the money and all the other things are in the boxes . . . what then?

2D Easy. Then Q and Shiner and Myra and Jack Smart all come . . . down . . . here . . . and . . . ulp!

Jack Smart enters with two money bags

Jack Smart That's it—the last. Put it in boxes, we'll be down as soon as possible for it all. Well done—you'll get what's coming to you!

Jack Smart exits

3D boxes up the money bags

2D Did you hear that? "Get what's coming to us." And you know what that means.

6D and 3D arrange the ten boxes along the table

Don't you care? Aren't you listening? What are we going to do now? Oh help!

6D Don't panic. We'll think of something. Just don't panic.

QH enters followed by 4D and 5D, each of whom carry boxes like those on stage that hold the trophies and other loot

QH Ah, there you are still. We'll need the blindfolds later of course, but meantime you can keep them off. Now just hold these boxes a moment will you . . . each one has a batch of tarts in it . . . ready for . . . for . . . for . . .

4D The judging!

QH Anything. That's the way!

4D and 5D hand over the boxes and go off for more

We can sort the order out later. We must ensure that it's all fair and . . . and . . . and . . .

2D Square.

QH . . . above board. My goodness me, it'll be the greatest event that we've ever had, I can hardly wait for my husband, Reginald, to arrive. He'll be the chief judge and . . . and . . . and . . .

4D and 5D return with the last of the boxed entries

5D Bottlewasher?

QH . . . you can be certain he will approve of all that I've done. He will be most impressed, I know it, and now if you'll just wait here and I must go and get myself . . . myself . . . myself . . .

4D Together?

5D An ice-cream?

3D Going?

6D Sorted out?

2D Ready?

QH Of course I am, dear boy. Let's hope you all are; this will be the event to end all . . . all . . . all . . . together . . .

2D ⎫
3D ⎪
4D ⎬ (*together*) Events!
5D ⎪
6D ⎭

QH Bless you!

QH sweeps out

6D And now what happens?

2D You mean you haven't thought of a way out for us? Oh dear, this really isn't good enough!

Q, Jack Flash, Jack Smart and Myra enter

Jack Smart There you are Q—what did I say?

Myra Worked like a dream.

Jack Flash And all ready in nice little boxes for us.

Q Ready for us to take away.

Jack Flash 'Ere—it's like a Chinese take-away cafe isn't it. But this time it's a fortune for us.

Myra Oh Jack, you are the clever one.

Jack Flash Thanks darling, I thought you'd never come round to my way of thinking.

Myra Not you, I mean my Jack Smart here.

Q Come on, there's no time to waste. We'll see the rest of you later.

Jack Flash (*sotto voce*) Much later!

Jack Smart Come on then.

Myra, Q, Jack Flash and Jack Smart take the boxes from the standing 2D, 3D, 4D, 5D and 6D and go out through the audience

Jack Smart Beautifully carried out.

Myra It was the plan, Jack, our plan.

Q I didn't think you had it in you, Smartie.

Jack Flash Pity about Jackson and the others, but by the time this lot's melted down . . .

They exit

4D Shouldn't we go after them?

5D What'll the Queen say?

2D She'll probably want to know who stole the . . . the . . . the . . .

3D Tarts?

They all laugh . . . and then stop suddenly

6D And what will we tell her?

Fanfare

4D Their Majesties the King and Queen of Hearts!

KH and QH enter escorted by guards, 6H and 7H, through the audience

KH and QH sit or stand on stage

QH Thank you, thank you, most loyal subjects. My husband and I are so pleased to be with you this evening, and now I call upon the judges to take their . . . their . . . their . . .

KH Places!

2D, 3D and 6D sit at their places

QH . . . time in coming to a decision in this important competition. The entries are before you and it will be your task to decide the . . . the . . . the . . .

KH Winner!
QH ... order of excellence. And so without any further ado, I ask you to sample the contents of the first ... first ... first ...
KH Box!
QH ... entrant!

Pause: 2D, 3D and 6D don't know how to play it

KH What's the delay? Come, come. What's the ...
QH Problem?
KH Don't interrupt, dear! Now come along, you judges ... you must eat some of what is in box number one. Do you understand?
6D Yes, your Majesty!
KH Then do it! Do it! Open the box for them.

4D opens a box

KH Take out the contents and hand them round.

4D takes out a trophy and is amazed

QH Good heavens, Reginald. What does this mean? What on earth are the ... the ... the ... (*She carries on stuttering "the ... the ... the" under the next*)
KH Open the next box.

4D does so, with the same result

And the next. And the next. And the next. And the next. And the next. And the next.
QH ... they doing in those boxes? And where are my tarts? Is no-one going to ... ex ... ex ... ex ...
KH Explode?
QH (*explosively*) ... explain! Explain!
6D If you'll allow me, your Majesties.
KH Can you explain all this?
6D I can, your Highness.
KH Quickly?
6D I hope so, your Highness.
6D These are the trophies and the medals for the big match today. And here is the ticket money. All have been stolen and were going to be taken away in these boxes by the thieves. However my friends and I here managed to deceive the thieves into taking the wrong boxes and instead of the gold and silver, all they have succeeded in stealing is ...
QH (*aghast*) My tarts!
6D Quite right, your Majesty.
KH And who are these thieves, who are these villains who have the tarts?
2D I'll tell you, your Majesty. It's ...

Q, Jack Smart, Jack Flash and Myra—enter down the aisles, before 2D can name names

Q Your Majesty, your Majesty. Are we too late?

KH Too late?

Q For the competition. We have our entries here.

KH *Your* entries.

Jack Smart Oh yes, your Majesty, we wanted so much to enter this competition and we have our entries here.

2D That's not true, your Highness. They are the thieves.

6D They stole the tarts, your Majesty.

3D And the trophies and the money.

Jack Flash Here are your tarts, your Majesty. We couldn't possibly be thieves . . . or we wouldn't have brought some entries for this competition, would we?

2D You fibbers! It's not true.

Myra We have the tarts to prove it.

6D Your Highness, it's not true what they say.

An argument between the two opposing opinions ensues: ad. libbed

KH Quiet! Quiet! All of you. Give me time to . . .

QH Well, I say it's a disgrace. Fancy bringing in entries at this late hour. It's . . . it's . . . it's . . .

KH Be quiet my dear. As I see it these people have brought the tarts to prove their case—they would hardly have come back if they were thieves would they? Now what evidence have you three to support *your* case?

6D Evidence?

3D Support?

2D Our *case*?

KH Without evidence in support of your story I find it all very hard to believe. Have you any evidence?

Q Your Majesty, it's obvious there is none. There is no proof whatsoever of their preposterous claim. Now may we leave our entries for the magnificent baking competition, and we could also return these trophies and the money to their rightful owners on the way.

KH Well . . .

6D Don't let them, your Majesty. It's all lies.

KH But where is your proof?

Pause

Well, since you can't provide proof, then I can do nothing but . . .

2D (*inspired*) Wait! (*He goes to the rear cupboards and opens them. Out spill Jackson, 10C and 4S*)

Jackson (*to Q*) Boss! Boss! I couldn't catch them. You'll have to delay the plan to pinch the trophies.

10C You'll never get away wiv it now 'cos we couldn't catch those others.

4S It's no good Shiner. We'll have to pinch the wotsits another time!

KH Now it's clear. Consider yourselves under arrest, you and your feeble assistants!

Cheers!

Take them away.

QH No! Wait! Wait! What about my competition? Who is going to ... to ... to ...

KH Judge?

QH ... to be the audience?

KH What's wrong with our present audience and our present judges for that matter? Take your seats again!

2D, 3D and 6D sit at their places

And now if you would taste the entries.

They taste the tarts

And your choice as the winner.

6D Our choice as winner is entry number six.

Applause

KH And who entered them?

4D (*turning over card*) Her Majesty, the Queen of Hearts.

QH Oh I've won! I've won!

KH Wait a moment my dear! *You* can't be the winner! You organized the competition.

QH But I entered them in someone else's ... someone else's ... someone else's ...

KH Oven?

QH ... name!

4D That's true your Majesty. They are entered in the names of the Two and Six of Diamonds.

2D |
6D | (*together, removing their disguises*) We've won. Hurray! It's us! We've won! It's us.

KH Quiet! Wait! You can't win—you were the judges. Now my dear ... who *really* made the tarts?

QH Well ...

KH Be honest.

QH It was my ... my ... my...

4D Cook, your Highness.

KH And who is your cook my dear?

5D I am, your Highness!

KH Well done! And your prize is a magnificent world cruise all expenses paid ... for four of you.

Comments all round "Four?"

So who will be going with you?

5D Er ... well, there's the Four of Diamonds, and the Three, and that means there's room for one more ... er ... er ...

2D (*putting up hand*) Me! Me!

5D (*to 6D*) And well, what about you?

6D I'd love to come. Thanks very much.

2D What about me? I'm left out again! Oh it's not fair. I'm the only one not to go.

Pause. 2D plays for sympathy

KH Well ... I think perhaps, under the circumstances we could make the prize—a trip for all five of you!

Pause

2D You mean it? I'm not left out? I'm going with you. Little me?
Myra Oh, stop moaning about it. You've won. What more d'you want?
All Don't mix it Myra!
2D And finally I'd just like to say three cheers for our side! Hip ... Hip ...
All Hoorah!

Three cheers end the play as the villains are escorted out

CURTAIN

FURNITURE AND PROPERTY LIST

ACT I

On stage: Cupboards labelled with hearts, clubs, diamonds and spades
Boxes (inside cupboard)
Bench/es
Newspaper

Personal: **Jackson:** cosh
6D: head bandage

ACT II

On stage: Bar with glasses, drinks
Several tables
Door
Leaflets

Personal: **2D:** false beard, cloak, floppy hat
6D: spades for disguise
4D: 2 entry forms
Jackson, 10C, 2S: shirts with long sleeves
6D: shirt and jacket with lapels
2D
6D } Joker outfits

ACT III

On stage: As Act I

Off stage: Table with cloth **(4D & 5D)**
Boxes with tarts inside **(4D and 5D)**
Cards with contestant's names **(4D and 5D)**

Personal: **2D, 3D, 6D:** blindfolds, rope
Jack Smart: trophies, medals, money bags

LIGHTING PLOT

Property fittings required: nil

One interior setting. One interior/exterior setting—entrance and interior to Bridge Club

ACT I

To open: General lighting

No cues

ACT II

To open: General lighting

No cues

ACT III

To open: General lighting

No cues

EFFECTS PLOT
ACT I

No cues

ACT II

No cues

ACT III

Cue 1   **6D:** "And what will we tell her?" ·   (Page 39)
             Fanfare